Explanations and Implications of the 1997 Amendments to IDEA

Rud Turnbull
University of Kansas

Melissa Cilley
Attorney-at-Law

Merrill,
an imprint of Prentice Hall

Upper Saddle River, New Jersey   Columbus, Ohio

Editor: Ann Castel Davis
Production Editor: JoEllen Gohr
Cover Designer: Diane C. Lorenzo
Cover art: © Photodisk, Inc.
Production Manager: Laura Messerly
Electronic Text Management: Marilyn Wilson Phelps
Director of Marketing: Kevin Flanagan
Marketing Manager: Suzanne Stanton
Marketing Coordinator: Krista Groshong

© 1999 by Prentice-Hall, Inc.
Upper Saddle River, New Jersey 07458

Printed in the United States of America

10 9 8 7 6

ISBN: 0-13-979527-8

INTRODUCTION

Nearly everyone has heard "the buzz" about the Individuals with Disabilities Education Act (IDEA): It was amended in 1997 and all of its provisions take effect on July 1, 1998. But what is behind "the buzz"? What does IDEA, as amended, really provide? To answer that question, one really has to ask three other questions:

1. What are IDEA's governing principles?
2. What are the specific provisions in the law that implement these principles?
3. What is the significance of the provisions, especially those that Congress added by the 1997 amendments?

Explanations and Implications of the 1997 Amendments to IDEA answers these three questions by giving you an organizing framework for understanding IDEA. Specifically, the text does the following:

- Part 1 describes the national policy that IDEA establishes and IDEA's major purposes.
- Part 2 it describes IDEA's six principles governing the education of students with disabilities—zero reject, nondiscriminatory evaluation, appropriate education, least restrictive environment, procedural due process, and parental and student participation.
- It quotes exactly or precisely paraphrases each provision of IDEA.
- It states, in language understandable to teachers, administrators, and parents, the import and impact of each provision.

One word of caution: This text is based on IDEA as amended in 1997, but it does **not** incorporate the 1998 regulations implementing IDEA. Those regulations, which are to promulgated by the U.S. Department of Education, Office of the Special Education and Rehabilitative Services, are not yet published as of the final writing of this text. So, for further understanding of IDEA and especially its implementation, you will want to refer to the regulations and, in particular, to the "notes" that accompany the regulation.

For Further Information

If you interested in a fuller explanation of IDEA and the court decisions that preceded the 1997 amendments and that seem likely to survive them, please refer to *Free Appropriate Public Education*, 5th Ed. (1998) by H. R. Turnbull and A. P. Turnbull and published by Love Publishing Company.

If you want to know how to implement IDEA for students in the schools, please refer to *Exceptional Lives: Special Education in Today's Schools*, 2nd Ed. (1999) by Turnbull, Turnbull, Shank, and Leal and published by Merrill/Prentice Hall. This book references the 1997 amendments and focuses on the inclusion and collaboration techniques that IDEA commands. The text is organized by the categories of disabilities that IDEA references in its definition of "children with disabilities."

And if you want to know how to practice state of the art collaboration between educators and families, please refer to *Families, Professionals, and Exceptionality*, 3rd Ed. (1998) by A.P. Turnbull and H.R. Turnbull and also published by Merrill/Prentice Hall. This book explains the techniques of educator-family collaboration and advocates empowerment for educators and families through collaboration.

PART ONE—OVERVIEW

I. National Policy and Nature of Individuals with Disabilities Education Act (20 U.S.C. Sections 1400 - 1487), as amended by P.L. 105-17 in 1997

A. National Policy, Section 1400(c)(1):

"Disability is a natural part of the human experience and in no way diminishes the right of individuals to participate in or contribute to society. Improving educational results for children with disabilities is an essential element of our national policy of ensuring equality of opportunity, full participation, independent living, and economic self-sufficiency for individuals with disabilities."

⌘ *Significance:* Here, Congress sets out four national policy goals: equal opportunity, full participation, independent living, and economic self-sufficiency. IDEA and special education are the means for helping students with disabilities achieve these goals.

B. Nature of IDEA

1. The Act authorizes federal funds to assist and induce state education agencies (SEAs) and local education agencies (LEAs) to change their policies and practices in order to carry out the Act's purposes and achieve the four national policy goals.

2. State (SEA) eligibility, Section 1412:
   Any state wanting federal aid under IDEA must apply for funding to the Secretary of Education. Eligibility is based on a showing that the state can meet all the provisions specifically set out by the law under Section 1412. Should the state meet all the provisions, funding will flow through the SEA.

3. Local (LEA) eligibility, Section 1413:
   In order for the SEA's federal funding to "pass-through" to the LEA, the LEA must file with the SEA once every three years. The filing must include a showing that the LEA can and will comply with the specific guidelines set out in Section 1413.

⌘ *Significance:* These provisions are the classic "carrot and stick" approach: federal funds are available only if the SEAs and LEAs agree to comply with IDEA.

II. Major Purposes of IDEA

A. **IDEA identifies barriers that have prevented children with disabilities from being educated effectively. These barriers have existed in spite of the fact that IDEA was first enacted in 1975. Under the 1997 Amendments, Congress tries to overcome these barriers.**

   1. Section 1400(C)(4): "[T]he implementation of this Act has been impeded by low expectations, and an insufficient focus on applying replicable research on proven methods of teaching and learning for children with disabilities."

   2. The proposed rules (regulations) carrying out IDEA identify five problems (Proposed Rule, p. 55028):

      a. Too many students with disabilities are dropping out of school.

      b. When students with disabilities drop out, they are less likely to ever return to school and are more likely to be unemployed or have problems with the law.

      c. Too many students with disabilities are failing courses.

      d. Almost half the students with disabilities do not participate in statewide assessments and, therefore, schools are not held accountable for results.

      e. Students from minority backgrounds continue to be placed disproportionately in separate special education settings. Proposed Rules, pg. 55028.

B. **IDEA identifies seven solutions to these barriers and, by specific provisions of the Act, attempts to put them into place. As set out in Section 1400(C)(5), the solutions are the following:**

   "Over 20 years of research and experience has demonstrated that the education of children with disabilities can be made more effective by"—

   1. "having high expectations for such children and ensuring their access in the general curriculum to the maximum extent possible;"

   2. "strengthening the role of parents and ensuring that families of such children have meaningful opportunities to participate in the education of their children at school and at home";

3. "coordinating this Act with other local, educational service agency, State, and Federal school improvement efforts in order to ensure that such children benefit from such efforts and that special education can become a service for such children rather than a place where they are sent";

4. "providing appropriate special education and relates services and aids and supports in the regular classroom to such children, whenever appropriate";

5. "supporting high-quality, intensive professional development for all personnel who work with such children in order to ensure that they have the skills and knowledge necessary to enable them—

   a. to meet developmental goals and, to the maximum extent possible, those challenging expectations that have been established for all children; and

   b. to be prepared to lead productive, independent, adult lives, to the maximum extent possible";

6. providing incentives for whole-school approaches and pre-referral intervention to reduce the need to label children as disabled in order to address their learning needs; and

7. focusing resources on teaching and learning while reducing paperwork and requirements that do not assist in improving educational results.

C. **In order to carry out the national policy goals, IDEA itself has several discrete purposes (Section 1400(d)):**

1. "to ensure that all children with disabilities have available to them a free appropriate public education that emphasizes special education and relates services resigned to meet their unique needs and prepare them for employment and independent living;

2. to ensure that the rights of children with disabilities and parents of such children are protected;

3. to assist States, localities, educational service agencies, and Federal agencies to provide for the education of all children with disabilities;

4. to assist States in the implementation of a statewide, comprehensive, coordinated, multidisciplinary, interagency system of early intervention services for infants and toddlers with disabilities and their families;

3

5. to ensure that educators and parents have the necessary tools to improve educational results for children with disabilities by supporting systematic-change activities; coordinated research and personnel preparation; coordinated technical assistance, dissemination, and support; and technology development and media services; and

6. to assess, and ensure the effectiveness of, efforts to educate children with disabilities."

D. As a general framework for carrying out the national policies and the IDEA purposes, IDEA creates Six Principles (which we discuss in detail below). These constitute a framework for the entire Act:

1. Zero Reject—a rule of educating all students and excluding none

2. Nondiscriminatory Evaluation—a rule of fair evaluation to determine whether a student has a disability and, if so, what the student's education should consist of

3. Appropriate Education—a rule of individualized education that benefits the student in making progress toward the national policy goals

4. Least Restrictive Placement/Environment—a rule that students with disabilities must, to the maximum extent appropriate for each one, be educated with students who do not have disabilities (their education being in the academic, extracurricular, and other school activities that nondisabled students participate in)

5. Procedural Due Process—a rule that allows the schools and the parents to resolve their differences by mediation and, if not by that means, by having hearings before impartial hearing officers or judges

6. Parent and Student Participation—a rule of shared decision-making, where educators, parents, and students collaborate in deciding what the student's education should consist of

⌘ *Significance:* These six principles are the framework for IDEA; we discuss them in detail below.

III. Definitions—IDEA defines its key terms with a good deal of particularity, and we set out below the most frequently used of those terms, using the definitions of Section 1401.

A. **"Assistive technology device":** means virtually any item, regardless of its origin, that is used to "increase, maintain, or improve functional capacity of a child with a disability."

⌘ *Significance:* This is the same definition used in the Technology-Assistance for Individuals with Disabilities Act ("the Tech Act") and in the Rehabilitation Act.

B. In general: "Child with a disability" refers to a child

1. "with mental retardation, hearing impairments (including deafness), speech or language impairments, visual impairments (including blindness), serious emotional disturbance (hereinafter referred to as 'emotional disturbance'), orthopedic impairments, autism, traumatic brain injury, other health impairments, or specific learning disabilities; and

2. who, by reason thereof, needs special education and related services."

⌘ *Significance:* This definition combines the "categorical" approach (listing the various categories of disabilities) with the "functional approach" (insisting that the disability cause the student to function in a way that requires special education intervention).

3. Child ages 3 through 9: The term 'child with a disability' for a child ages 3 through 9 may, at the discretion of the State and the local educational agency, include a child

   a. experiencing developmental delays, as defined by the State and as measured by appropriate diagnostic instruments and procedures, in one or more of the following areas: physical development, cognitive development, communication development, social or emotional development, or adaptive development; and

   b. who, by reason thereof, needs special education and relates services."

⌘ *Significance:* This provision allows, but does not require, a state to serve "at risk" students. These students have not yet been identified as having a disability and needing special education; they are not yet "classified" or "made eligible" for special education. Nonetheless, because they are at risk for being classified into special education, the state may serve them in an effort to prevent them from being classified into special education. This is a way of preventing special education placement.

C. "Free appropriate public education means special education and related services that—

1. have been provided at public expense, under public supervision and direction, and without charge;

2. meet the standards of the State educational agency

3. include an appropriate preschool, elementary, or secondary school education in the State involved; and

4. are provided in conformity with the individualized education program required under Section 1414(d)."

⌘ *Significance:* No change from prior law.

D. **"Parent"** includes a legal guardian and generally includes an individual assigned to be a surrogate parent.

⌘ *Significance:* No change from prior law.

E. **"Related services" means** "transportation, and such developmental, corrective, and other supportive services (including speech-language pathology and audiology services, psychological services, physical and occupational therapy, recreation, including therapeutic recreation, social work services, counseling services, including rehabilitation counseling, orientation and mobility services, and medical services, except that such medical services shall be for diagnostic and evaluation purposes only) as may be required to assist a child with a disability to benefit from special education, and includes the early identification and assessment of disabling conditions in children."

⌘ *Significance:* A related service is available by right only if a child "needs" it; the test is one of necessity, as under prior law. Orientation and mobility training was added by the 1997 amendments.

F. **"Special education** means specially designed instruction, at no cost to parents, to meet the unique needs of a child with a disability, including—

1. instruction conducted in the classroom, in the home, in hospitals and institutions, and in other settings; and

2. instruction in physical education."

⌘ *Significance:* No change from prior law.

G. "Specific learning disability"

1. In general the term 'specific learning disability' means a disorder in one or more of the basic psychological processes involved in understanding or in using language, spoken or written, which disorder may manifest itself in imperfect ability to listen, thin, speak, read, write, spell, or do mathematical calculations.

2. Disorders included: The term includes such conditions as perceptual disabilities, brain injury, minimal brain dysfunction, dyslexia, and developmental aphasia.

3. Disorders excluded: The term does not include "a learning problem that is primarily the result of visual, hearing, or motor disabilities, of mental retardation, of emotional disturbance, or of environmental, cultural, or economic disadvantage."

⌘ *Significance:* No change from prior law; the definition uses an "inclusionary" approach (paragraphs 1 and 2) and an exclusionary approach (paragraph 3).

H. **"Supplementary aids and services"** means "aids, services, and other supports that are provided in regular education classes or other education-related settings to enable children with disabilities to be educated with nondisabled children to the maximum extent appropriate in accordance with Section 1412(a)(5)."

⌘ *Significance:* No change from prior law.

I. **"Transition services"** means "a coordinated set of activities for a student with a disability that—

1. is designed within an outcome-oriented process, which promotes movement from school to post-school activities, including post-secondary education, vocational training, integrated employment (including supported employment), continuing and adult education, adult services, independent living, or community participation;

2. is based upon the individual student's needs, taking into account the student's preferences and interests; and

3. includes instruction, related services, community experiences, the development of employment and other post-school adult living objectives, and, when appropriate, acquisition of daily living skills and functional vocational evaluation."

⌘ *Significance:* No change from prior law.

7

PART TWO—SIX PRINCIPLES

I. Overview

As stated above, the "six principles" constitute a framework for IDEA. So many people fail to understand IDEA wholly and conceptually because they lack a framework. With the framework of the six principles, however, all of IDEA makes sense as a sensible, seamless approach to educating students with disabilities.

The first four of these six principles reflect the actual process that schools follow and that students with disabilities and their families encounter; the last two are the ways in which the schools are held accountable for carrying out the first four principles.

- **zero reject** reflects the process of enrollment;

- **nondiscriminatory evaluation** occurs after the student enters school and when the school or others believe the student may have a disability and be entitled to IDEA's benefits;

- **appropriate education** occurs when the student receives individualized programs that benefit him/her in progressing toward the national policy goals;

- **least restrictive environment** reflects the presumption that the student's education will take place in a typical setting and with nondisabled students;

- **procedural due process** is a way for parents to holds the school accountable for that education and for the schools to hold the parents accountable to their child;

- **parent participation** ensures that the parents and the student collaborate with educators in having a say about the student's education.

⌘ *Significance:* These principles create a seamless framework for educating students with disabilities. Each and every student with a disability is enrolled and none is excluded. Each receives a nondiscriminatory evaluation that becomes the basis for the student's appropriate education and for placement in the least restrictive educational program. If the schools or parents do not carry out IDEA, procedural due process gives them a chance to hold the other accountable for appropriately educating the student. In order to assure that the schools and parents and students will carry out the first four principles, the participation principle insists on shared decision-making.

II. The Zero Reject Principle: "Nothing is clearer in IDEA than Congress's intent to include all children with disabilities in school and to require all state agencies to follow a policy of zero reject" [Turnbull & Turnbull, Free Appropriate Public Education (1998, p. 45)]. IDEA adopts several different strategies to carry out the zero reject principle.

A. Ages covered (3-21), Section 1412(a)(2)(A): All students with disabilities, from ages 3 through 21, are entitled to a free appropriate public education.

Note: The term "all" includes even those students who, in the judgment of some people, seem to be "ineducable." In 1988, *Timothy W. v. Rochester School District* held that IDEA was enacted to ensure that all children with disabilities are provided an appropriate education. The court focused on the state's responsibility to the child, noting that Congress never intended to exclude any student; even if a student seems to be so impaired that he cannot learn anything, the student still has the right to receive services from the SEA or LEA. The 1997 amendments restate the zero-reject foundation created by *Timothy W.* by requiring states to provide full educational opportunities to **all** children with disabilities between the ages of 3 and 21, Section 1412(a)(2)(A).

⌘ *Significance:* "All" means all. This requirement refuses to allow any group of children or any individual child to "slip through the cracks."

B. Early intervention (0-3) [Part C]:

1. Under Section 1437, a state may choose to provide services to infants and toddlers (birth/0 to 3) and their families. If it chooses to provide these services, it can receive federal funds under IDEA's early intervention provisions.

2. Early intervention is outcome-oriented and result-focused, for its purposes (Section 1413(a)) are

   a. to enhance the development of infants and toddlers with disabilities and to minimize their potential for developmental delay;

   b. to reduce the educational costs to our society, including our Nation's schools, by minimizing the need for special education and related services after infants and toddlers with disabilities reach school age;

   c. to minimize the likelihood of institutionalization of individuals with disabilities and maximize the potential for their independently living in society;

d.   to enhance the capacity of families to meet the special needs of
        their infants and toddlers with disabilities; and

   e.   to enhance the capacity of the State and local agencies and
        service providers to identify, evaluate, and meet the needs of
        historically underrepresented populations, particularly
        minority, low-income, inner-city, and rural populations.

⌘ *Significance:* Early intervention is a preventive strategy that provides
services for the child as well as the family in the critical early years of the
child's life—from birth to age three.

   C. Transition planning: In order to assure that infants and toddlers will
        make a smooth transition from early intervention (0 to 3 years) to early
        childhood (3 to 5 years), Section 1412 (a)(9) requires a transition plan
        for them, consisting of interagency cooperation (early intervention and
        early childhood education in cooperation with each other) and an
        individualized education program, to be developed and implemented by
        the child's third birthday.

⌘ *Significance:* Transition planning is a proactive initiative intended to
provide a seamless transition from family-related services to education-
related services.

   D. Comprehensive coverage: In order to reach every child who has a
        disability, without regard to the nature of the educational or other
        system that serves the child, Section 1412 entitles students in religious
        schools, private schools, and cluster schools to receive all of IDEA's
        benefits.

Note: The SEA or LEA does not violate the Federal Constitution's rule
against "establishing" a religion when it provides related services to a
student on the premises of a parochial school, *Zobrest v. Catalina Foothills
School District* (1993). The 1997 amendments to IDEA codifies this
decision:

    "To the extent consistent with the number and location of children with
disabilities in the State who are enrolled by their parents in private
elementary and secondary schools, provision is made for the participation of
those children in the program assisted or carried out under this part by
providing for such children special education and related services in
accordance with the following requirements, unless the Secretary has
arranged for services to those children:

        *Amounts expended for the provision of those services by a local
educational agency shall be equal to proportionate amount of Federal
funds made available under this part.

*Such services may be provided to children with disabilities on the premises of private, including parochial, schools, to the extent consistent with law." Section 1412(a)(10)(A)(i)(I)-(II).

Note: The local educational agency must serve students attending charter schools in the same manner as students attending any other school; and the local educational agency must also provide funds to charter school as any other school. See Section 1413(a)(5).

⌘ *Significance:* Through its provisions related to parochial, private, and charter schools, IDEA allows parents to chose where to send their child and does not require the parents to run the risk that their child will lose the benefits of IDEA simply because of a placement into one of these kinds of schools.

E. **Direct services by State educational agency, Section 1413(h):** When an LEA fails to provide appropriate services to its students, the SEA must remedy the default by providing services directly to those students, using the funds that the LEA otherwise would have received.

⌘ *Significance:* This section makes it possible for students in a defaulting LEA to get IDEA services from the SEA directly.

F. **Single-agency responsibility, Section 1412(a)(11):**

1. The SEA is the state agency ultimately responsible for assuring that IDEA's requirements are carried out throughout the entire state.

2. The SEA is responsible for interagency coordination to ensure that all students receive a free appropriate public education, including those served by other state agencies, such as the state's mental health, developmental disabilities, or juvenile justice agencies.

⌘ *Significance:* As with the "direct services" provision, this provision assures that each student, wherever served, will receive IDEA's benefits.

G. **Costs and cost-shifting:** The 1997 amendments allow for some of the costs of special education and related services to be "shifted" to or shared among other public agencies.

1. Section 1412(a)(23)(A) requires the SEA to assure that there is in effect "an interagency agreement or other mechanism for interagency coordination...between each public agency...and the State educational agency, in order to ensure that all services...that are needed to ensure a free appropriate public education are provided..."

2. Section 1412(a)(23)(A)(i) requires that "the financial responsibility of each public agency..., including the State Medicaid agency and other public insurers of children with disabilities, shall precede the financial responsibility of the local educational agency...."

3. Section 1412(a)(23)(B)(i) requires all public agencies to fulfill their IDEA duties; if they do not, the SEA may carry out those duties and seek reimbursement for the costs of doing what the other agencies should have done.

❀ *Significance:* These provisions assure that all agencies that have students with disabilities in their service systems must provide those students the benefits of IDEA; they create a "first/last" payor system (other agencies pay first, the SEA pays last); and they spread the costs of special education and related services across more agencies than just the SEA, thus providing greater education-related funding overall.

H. Child Census: Section 1412 requires the SEA to assure that there will be an annual census of students with disabilities:

"All children with disabilities residing in the State, including children with disabilities attending private schools, regardless of the severity of their disabilities, and who are in need of special education and related services, are identified, located, and evaluated and a practical method is developed and implemented to determine which children with disabilities are currently receiving needed special education and related services."

❀ *Significance:* This is a gap-closing provision that ensures that no children are denied a free appropriate public education because they are difficult to locate or serve.

I. Architectural barriers, Section 1404:

The Secretary of Education may make grants to SEAs "to be used to acquire appropriate equipment, or to construct new facilities or alter existing facilities" to bring them into compliance with the 'Americans with Disabilities Accessibility Guidelines for Buildings and Facilities.'

❀ *Significance:* Without this section, zero-reject may be impossible because of architectural barriers that prohibit certain students from attending school.

J. Personnel:

1. Comprehensive System of Personnel Development (CSPD) (in-service training of SEA and LEA employees): Section 1412(a)(14) requires the SEA to assure that "the State has in effect...a comprehensive system of personnel development that is designed to ensure an adequate supply of qualified special education, regular education, and related services personnel..."

2. General standards: Section 1412(a)(15)(A) and (B) requires the SEA to set the standards that SEA and LEA employees must meet to get or retain their jobs.

3. Paraprofessionals and assistants: Section 1412(a)(15)(B)(iii) permits the SEA and LEAs to employ them if they are appropriately trained.

4. Personnel vacancies: Section 1412(a)(15)(C) requires the SEA to require LEAs to make ongoing good faith efforts to satisfy personnel needs.

⌘ *Significance:* These sections assure that there will be a sufficient number of appropriately trained SEA and LEA personnel to carry out IDEA. The personnel include special and general educators and related service providers. Without these personnel, IDEA would make no real difference to the students; they would experience "exclusion" just as much as if they were not in school at all.

K. **Students in correctional facilities:**

1. Juvenile Offenders Treated as Adults: Section 1412(a)(1)(B)(ii) excludes from IDEA's benefits those juveniles who are incarcerated in an adult facility and who were not identified as entitled to special education and did not have an IEP before they were incarcerated.

2. Other Juvenile Offenders: Section 1414(d)(6) limits some of the IDEA rights of students with disabilities who were identified as entitled to special education and who had an IEP before they were incarcerated. They do not have the right to participate in SEA or LEA assessments or to be provided transition programs if they will be over 21 when released from state custody; and, if the SEA can demonstrate a "bona fide security or compelling penological interest that cannot otherwise be accommodated," the SEA may modify the IEP safeguards and the rules for placing the student in the least restrictive environment.

3. SEA Responsibility: The Governor may assign to a state agency other than the SEA the duties of carrying out IDEA for the benefit of students in state custody, Section 1412(a)(11)(C).

⌘ *Significance:* These provisions take into account that there are bona fide penological reasons to restrict the IDEA rights of some students. At the same time, these provisions allow them to receive some of IDEA's benefits, consistent with the state's interest in confining, punishing, and rehabilitating them.

L. Expulsion and Discipline:

1. In *Honig v. Doe,* 484 U.S. 305 (1988), the United States Supreme Court held that an LEA may not expel a student if the student's behavior that triggered the discipline was a manifestation of the student's disability. IDEA codifies that decision and adds new protections for the student and for others in school (out of concern for school safety).

2. "A free appropriate public education is available to all children with disabilities residing in the State between the ages of 3 and 21, inclusive, *including children with disabilities who have been suspended or expelled from school.*" Section 1412(a)(1)(emphasis added).

⌘ ***Significance:*** This provision is a rule against "cessation" of services. If a student has been suspended or expelled from school, the student still is entitled to IDEA's benefits and the LEA must continue to serve the student despite the suspension or expulsion.

3. Consistent with the *Honig* decision and Section 1412(a)(1), Section 1415(k) provides that a student whose behavior is a manifestation of a disability may be disciplined, but it creates discipline procedures that an LEA must follow and limits the type of discipline an LEA may impose.

   a. Under Section 1415(k)(5)(B), a student whose behavior is not a manifestation of a disability may be disciplined just as any nondisabled student may be disciplined.

⌘ ***Significance:*** If the student's disability did not cause the behavior, then the student is "nondisabled" for the purpose of discipline and may be dealt with as any nondisabled student may be dealt with. This is an "equal treatment" approach.

   b. However, as noted above, Section 1412(a)(1)(A) prohibits the cessation of services; this is a "more than equal treatment" approach.

   c. Section 1415(k)(5)(B) provides that if an LEA initiates disciplinary procedures, it must ensure that the student's special education and disciplinary records are transmitted to the person who is responsible for the discipline of nondisabled students.

⌘ ***Significance:*** This provision requires the LEA to transmit records to the discipline-imposing authorities so they will know and be able to take into account the student's disability and prior "record" (in mitigation or not of the discipline to be imposed).

    d.   Short-term suspensions—the 10-day rule: Section 1415(k)(1) allows for short-term (not more than 10 days) changes of placement to an appropriate interim educational setting, another setting, or suspension, but only if those alternatives may be applied to children without disabilities.

⌘ *Significance:* The *Honig* case allowed for short-term (10-day) suspensions, a sort of "cooling off" period.

    e.   Long-term discipline (more than 10 days) and manifestation reviews, Section 1415(k)(4):

"If a disciplinary action is contemplated (where the student carries a weapon to school or possesses or uses illegal drugs or if the child's current placement is substantially likely to result in injury to the child or others)...or if a disciplinary action involving a change of placement for more than 10 days is contemplated for a child with a disability who has engaged in other behavior that violated any rule or code of conduct of the local education agency that applies to all children—

    i.   not later than the date on which the decision to take that action is made, the parents shall be notified of that decision and of all procedural safeguards...; and

    ii.   immediately, if possible, but in no case later than 10 school days after the date on which the decision to take that action is made, a review shall be conducted of the relationship between the child's disability and the behavior subject to the disciplinary action."

⌘ *Significance:* This provision requires a hearing to determine whether there is a manifestation (disability causes behavior). The manifestation hearing must be held in cases of (a) weapons, (b) drugs, (c) dangerous behavior, and (d) any discipline for more than 10 days.

    f.   Manifestation Review Team: Section 1415(k)(4)(B) provides that the IEP team and "other qualified personnel" shall carry out a manifestation review.

⌘ *Significance:* The IEP team, plus others, know the student; they were the team that evaluated the student and prepared the student's educational program (IEP) and made the student's placement decision. They are the ones best qualified to determine "manifestation."

g. Conduct of Manifestation Review: Section 1415(k)(4)(C) provides that the IEP team "may determine that the behavior of the child was not a manifestation of the child's disability only if the IEP Team—

  i. "first considers, in terms of the behavior subject to disciplinary action, all relevant information, including—

    *evaluation and diagnostic results, including such results or other relevant information supplied by the parents of the child;

    *observations of the child; and

    *the child's IEP and placement; and

  ii. then determines that—

    *in relationship to the behavior subject to disciplinary action, the child's IEP and placement were appropriate and the special education services, supplementary aids and services, and behavior intervention strategies were provided consistent with the child's IEP and placement;

    *the child's disability did not impair the ability of the child to understand the impact and consequences of the behavior subject to disciplinary action; and

    *the child's disability did not impair the ability of the child to control the behavior subject to disciplinary action."

⌘ *Significance:* The team must consider specified evidence that may or may not point to manifestation. It also must consider the "defenses" that the student may raise against any discipline (these being that the LEA defaulted in its IEP duties, the student had a cognitive impairment, or the student had a behavioral impairment).

h. Parent Appeal: Section 1415(k)(6) provides that "If the child's parent disagrees with a determination that the child's behavior was not a manifestation of the child's disability or with any decision regarding placement, the parent may request a hearing." The LEA must provide for an "expedited" hearing (if the parent asks for one) and at the hearing the hearing officer "shall determine whether the (LEA) has demonstrated that the child's behavior was not a manifestation of the child's disability."

M. Stay-Put

1. The 1997 amendments also codify the holding in *Honig* regarding the stay-put rule.

2. Thus, Section 1415(j) provides that "[D]uring the pendency of any proceedings conducted pursuant to this section, unless the State or local educational agency and the parents otherwise agree, the child shall remain in the then-current educational placement of such child, or, if applying for initial admission to a public school, shall, with the consent of the parents, be placed in the public school program until all such proceedings have been completed."

   a. The local educational agency may, however, change the student's placement to an appropriate interim alternative educational setting, another setting, or suspend student for up to ten days, Section 1415(k)(1)(A). The student has no right to services during this period, consistent with the *Honig* case and the "cooling off" theory.

   b. If a student is subjected to change of placement into an interim alternative educational setting, another setting, or is suspended, and if the student's parents challenge the school's decision to impose any of the three disciplinary changes in placement, the stay-put rule goes into effect following the 10-day period and the student stays in his/her current placement. The "current placement" is "the child's placement prior to the interim alternative setting", Section 1415(k)(1)(A).

   c. The 10-day period includes every short-term suspension in a given school year. If the student is suspended for five days and then suspended again a month later for seven days, that student has been suspended cumulatively for twelve days over the entire school year and the protections listed above go into effect, Section 1415(k)(1)(A)(i).

   d. There is no requirement for a manifestation determination review or a functional behavioral assessment if cumulative suspension equals less than 10 days.

   e. Parents must receive notice and may appeal through an expedited hearing, Section 1415(k)(6)(A).

3. Exceptions to the Stay-Put Rule

   a. Weapons and drugs—the first exception to the stay-put rule: Under Section 1415(k)I1)(A)(iii),

    i.   A student may be placed into an interim alternative educational setting for up to 45 days if

          *"the child carries a weapon to school or to a school function...or

          *the child knowingly possesses or uses illegal drugs or sells or solicits the sale of a controlled substance while at school or a school function."

⌘ *Significance:* This provision balances school safety against the student's IDEA rights; placement into the IAES is allowed but within the IAES the student continues to get IDEA benefits.

    ii.   The interim alternative educational setting "must be selected so as to enable the child to continue to participate in the general curriculum, although in another setting, and to continue to receive those services and modifications, including those described in the child's current IEP, that will enable the child to meet the goals set out in that IEP", Section 1415(k)(3)(B).

⌘ *Significance:* The IAES is "interim" and thus should not disrupt the student's IEP and IDEA rights.

    b.   Dangerous behavior—the second exception to the stay-put rule: Under Section 1415(k)(2), an LEA may seek permission from a due process hearing officer to place a student for up to 45 days into an interim alternative educational setting because of dangerousness. The hearing officer may order placement into the IAES only if the officer

    *"determines that the (LEA) has demonstrated by substantial evidence that maintaining the current placement of the child is substantially likely to result in injury to the child or others"

    *"considers the appropriateness of the child's current placement"

    *"considers whether the (LEA) has made reasonable efforts to minimize the risk of harm in the child's current placement, including the use of supplementary aids and services" and

    *determines that the IAES allows the child's IEP to be carried out

    4.   Preemptive Strike: Sometimes a student not yet classified into special education will claim that he/she is, in fact, a student with a disability and that the LEA may not discipline him/her except in accordance with IDEA. This is the "preemptive strike" that the

student makes against an LEA.

a. Section 1415(k)(8) provides the student may claim IDEA protections "if the (LEA) had knowledge ... that the child was a child with a disability before the behavior that precipitated the disciplinary action occurred."

b. Section 1415(k)(8) also provides that the LEA is charged with ("deemed to have") that knowledge if

   i. "the parent of the child has expressed concern in writing (unless the parent is illiterate or has a disability that prevents compliance with the requirements contained in this clause) to personnel of the appropriate educational agency that the child is in need of special education and related services;

   ii. the behavior or performance of the child demonstrates the need for such services;

   iii. the parent of the child has requested an evaluation pursuant to Section 1414; or

   iv. the teacher of the child, or other personnel of the local educational agency, has expressed concern about the behavior or performance of the child to the director of special education of such agency or to other personnel of the agency."

⌘ *Significance:* The LEA has to be careful to deal with students who may have disabilities (under the "deeming" provision) and it cannot escape providing them with IDEA protection in discipline and IDEA benefits if, in fact, the student is entitled to be classified into IDEA.

N. **Behavioral Intervention and Supports, Section 1415(k)(1)(B):** When a student is subject to any kind of discipline other than the short-term 10-day suspension, the LEA must conduct develop a plan to deal with the student's behavior.

   1. If the LEA has not already conducted a "functional behavioral assessment" and implemented a "behavioral intervention plan" before disciplining the student, the IEP team must conduct an assessment and develop a plan.

   2. If the LEA, however, has conducted a functional behavioral assessment and developed a behavioral intervention plan, the IEP team must "review" and "modify" the plan, "as necessary, to address the behavior."

⌘ Significance: Discipline for more than 10 days triggers a functional assessment and behavioral intervention plan; thus, the behavior that caused the discipline will be addressed.

II.   Nondiscriminatory Evaluation

    A.   **The nondiscriminatory evaluation** must be performed by the persons who constitute the student's IEP team, Section 1414(d)(1)(B); and the evaluation has two essential purposes, Section 1414(c)(1)(B), namely

        1.   to determine "whether the child has a particular category of disability" (one of the listed categories: see "definitions") or, in the case of a reevaluation, "continues to have such a disability," and, if so,

        2.   to determine the consequences of that first determination, specifically,

            a.   the students' "present levels of performance and educational need,"

            b.   "whether the child needs special education and related services, or in the case of a reevaluation of a child, whether the child continues to need special education and related services, and

            c.   "whether any additions or modifications to the special education and related services are needed to enable the child to meet the measurable annual goals set out in the individualized education program of the child and to participate, as appropriate, in the general curriculum."

⌘ Significance: This section links the nondiscriminatory evaluation to the individualized education program and the student's placement by having the same people serve on the evaluation and on the IEP/placement teams and by making the evaluation's purposes explicit and requiring them to be connected to program and placement. Thus, evaluation is the basis for determining not only whether the student has a disability but also, if that is the case, what the school must do about the disability (namely, develop and carry out an appropriate education through the IEP and provide services in the least restrictive environment of the general curriculum).

    B.   **The team must adhere to specific standards, Section 1414(b), including those related to**

        1.   the student:

a. the test must be "selected and administered as not to be discriminatory on a racial or cultural basis." Section 1414(b)(3)(A)(i).

b. the test must be "provided and administered in child's native language or other mode of communication...." Section 1414(b)(3)(A)(ii).

c. the student must be evaluated with two purposes in mind, namely to determine "whether the child is a child with a disability and the content of the child's individualized education program, including information related to enabling the child to be involved in and progress in the general curriculum or, for preschool children, to participate in appropriate activities...." Section 1414(b)(2)(A).

2. the tests:

a. must "have been validated for the specific purpose for which they are used"

b. must be "administered by trained and knowledgeable personnel" and

c. must be "administered in accordance with any instructions provided by the producer of such tests."

3. the evaluation process must

a. include "a variety of assessment tools and strategies to gather relevant functional and developmental information, including information provided by the parent, that may assist" the team in making the two critical determinations (does the student have a disability; if so, what should the student's education consist of)

b. not rely on "any single procedure as the sole criterion for determining whether the child is a child with a disability or determining an appropriate educational program for the child;" and

c. "use technically sound instruments" to assess the student across four domains, namely, cognitive, behavioral, physical, and developmental

d. in conducting the initial and subsequent reevaluations, the IEP team shall

(i) "review existing evaluation data on the child, including evaluations and information provided by the parents of the child, current classroom-based assessments and observations, and teacher and related services providers observation," and

(ii) "on the basis of that review, and input from the child's parents, identify what additional data, if any, are needed..."

⌘ *Significance:* The nondiscriminatory evaluation procedures assure that the LEA will accurately identify the student as one who has a disability and then will develop an appropriate education (via the IEP and least restrictive placement) on the basis of the evaluation and on no other basis. Thus, the evaluation is the foundation for all that follows; it is the first element of a seamless educational process.

There are new provisions, namely the requirement to focus on four domains (cognitive, behavioral, physical, and developmental) and the requirement to consider existing evaluation data (and the option to not do a complete reevaluation each time some reevaluation has to be done).

C. **Special rule for eligibility determination, relating to nondisability factors, Section 1414(b)(5):** "...a child shall not be determined to be a child with a disability if the determinant factor for such determination is lack of instruction in reading or math or limited English proficiency."

⌘ *Significance:* This section provides assurances that children from minority groups or from educationally impoverished programs will not be made eligible for IDEA solely because of those factors. The section is concerned with the overrepresentation of minority students in special education and seeks to reduce their representation in special education.

D. **Parent participation, Section 1414(d)(1)(B):** The student's parent(s) must be member of the evaluation and IEP teams.

E. **Parent Consent, Section 1414(a)(1)(C):**

1. Any agency proposing to conduct an initial evaluation or subsequent evaluation must obtain the "informed consent" of the child's parent before the evaluation or reevaluation.

2. The parental consent applies only to that particular evaluation and "shall not be construed as consent for placement for receipt of special education and related services."

3. If the agency attempts to gain parental consent but receives no response, it must use the mediation or due process procedures to secure approval for an evaluation or reevaluation.

4. If the agency is proposing to conduct a reevaluation, it must secure parental consent, but if it cannot do so, it may proceed with the evaluation if it can "demonstrate that it had taken reasonable measures to obtain such consent and the child's parent has failed to respond."

⌘ *Significance:* Parent participation in the evaluation process is critical, assuring (a) collaborative decision-making, (b) parental involvement in the child's education, (c) parental information that aids the other members of the team, and (d) parental knowledge about whether the child has a disability and, if so, what the program and placement will be (with the evaluation as a foundation). With at least one parent as a member of the team and with IDEA's requirement for parental consent, the evaluation process can focus on each area of the child's needs and each area of concern for the parents.

F. **Reevaluation, Section 1414(a)(2):**

1. Reevaluation is warranted under three conditions:

   a. at least once every three years

   b. if "conditions warrant"

   c. if parents or teacher requests it.

2. Reevaluation requires parental consent, Section 1414(c)(3)

3. The evaluation/IEP team must comply with all initial evaluation standards and procedures, even when they are conducting the "exit" evaluation that precedes the student's discharge from special education or the student's leaving or graduating from school, Section 1414(c)(5).

4. During each reevaluation, Section 1414(c), the team must

   a. examine existing evaluation data,

   b. identify what additional data are needed,

   c. notify the child's parents that no new data are needed and why that is so (and no new evaluation is warranted),

   d. conduct new evaluations only upon parental request.

⌘ *Significance:* This section provides an opportunity for the LEA or the parents to request more testing if a child's needs appear unmet. This section also requires that the child be reevaluated periodically so any change in need will be identified and addressed.

     G. No Evaluation, No Services: An agency may not provide special education and related services without conducting a full and individual initial evaluation, Section 1414(a)(1).

⌘ *Significance:* This section ensures that a child who does not need special education will not be placed improperly in a special education setting. It also ensures that a child needing special education will not be misclassified and improperly served.

     H. Infants and Toddlers: The nondiscriminatory evaluation requirement extends to infants and toddlers (birth to three), Section 1435(a)(3).

⌘ *Significance:* This section protects infants and toddlers from misclassification.

III.   Appropriate Education

     A. Definition: Section 1401(8) defines the term "Free Appropriate Public Education" as: "Special education and related services that

       1.   have been provided at public expense, under public supervision and direction, and without charge;

       2.   meet the standards of the State educational agency;

       3.   include an appropriate preschool, elementary, or secondary school education in the State involved; and

       4.   are provided in conformity with the individualized education program."

     B. Rowley Decision: The U.S. Supreme Court's first special education decision, *Board of Education v. Rowley* (1982), defined "appropriate" and the 1997 amendments do nothing to change the Court's approach. The Court adopted a two-part definition. One part holds that "appropriate" consists of a program that provides the student with a reasonable opportunity to benefit. The second part holds that "appropriate" results from following IDEA's procedures (the "process" definition), specifically by conducting a nondiscriminatory evaluation, developing an individualized education program, attempting to place the child in the least restrictive appropriate program, assuring that the parents have access to the child's school records throughout this process, and convening a due process hearing if the parents wish to protest the placement or any other action related to the child's right to a free appropriate public education.

⌘ *Significance:* IDEA continues to define "appropriate" by requiring that the student benefit and that the IDEA process be followed. The keystones to "appropriate" are, of course, the nondiscriminatory evaluation (because it is the basis for the IEP) and the IEP (which is the basis for the student's curriculum, related services, supplementary aids and services) and placement in the least restrictive environment.

C. **Individualized education program (IEP), Section 1414(d).**

1. **The IEP is a "written statement** for each child with a disability that is developed, reviewed, and revised...and that includes

    a. a statement of the child's present levels of educational performance including

        i. how the child's disability affects the child's involvement and progress in the general curriculum; or

        ii. for preschool children, as appropriate, how the disability affects the child's participation in appropriate activities;

    b. a statement of measurable annual goals, including benchmarks or short-term objectives, related to

        i. meeting the child's needs that result from the child's disability to enable the child to be involved in and progress in the general curriculum; and

        ii. meeting each of the child's other educational needs that result from the child's disability;

    c. a statement of the special education and related services and supplementary aids and services to be provided to the child, or on behalf of the child, and a statement of the program modifications or supports for school personnel that will be provided for the child—

        i.   to advance appropriately toward attaining the annual goals;

        ii. to be involved and progress in the general curriculum...and to participate in extracurricular and other nonacademic activities; and

        iii. to be educated and participate with other children with disabilities and nondisabled children in [such] activities;

    d. an explanation of the extent, if any, to which the child will not participate with nondisabled children in the regular classroom and in the activities described [above];

e. a statement of

    i. any individual modifications in the administration of State or district-wide assessments of student achievement that are needed in order for the child to participate in such assessment and

    ii. if the IEP team determines that the child will not participate in a particular State or district-wide assessment of student achievement (or part of such an assessment), a statement of

    *why that assessment is not appropriate for the child; and

    *how the child will be assessed;

f. the projected date for the beginning of services and modifications..., and the anticipated frequency, location, and duration of those services and modifications;

g. beginning at age 14, and updated annually, *a statement of* the transition service needs of the child under the applicable components of the child's IEP that focuses on the child's courses of study (such as participation in advanced-placement courses or a vocational education program);

h. beginning at age 16 (or younger, if determined appropriate by the IEP team), *a statement of* needed transition services for the child, including, when appropriate, a statement of the interagency responsibilities or any needed lineages;

i. beginning at least one year before the child reaches the age of majority under State law, a statement that the child has been informed of his or her rights under this title, if any, that will transfer to the child on reaching the age of majority...; and

j. a statement of

    i. how the child's progress toward the annual goals...will be measured; and

    ii. how the child's parents will be regularly informed (by such means as periodic report cards), at least as often as parents are informed of their nondisabled children's progress, of—

*their child's progress toward annual goals...; and

*the extent to which that progress is sufficient to enable the child to achieve the goals by the end of the year. Section 1414(d)(1)(A) emphasis added.

⌘ *Significance:* The IEP is now explicitly connected with and serves as the nexus between the nondiscriminatory evaluation, the student's program, and the student's least restrictive environment placement ("involvement and progress in the general curriculum"). This was so under earlier court interpretations of IDEA, but IDEA now outlines a much more explicit and detailed connection between the evaluation, program, and placement.

The IEP provisions are significant for other reasons, too:

*they emphasize access to the general curriculum;

*they secure accountability by identifying present educational levels and measurable annual goals, by presuming that the student will participate in state and local assessments (and thus be "measured" according to how he/she is doing relative to other students), and by requiring schools to notify parents (as often as they notify parents of nondisabled students) about their child's progress;

*they presume that the student will participate in these assessments and require the IEP team to justify the student's exclusion and to identify accommodations so the student can participate in the assessments;

*they assure related services and supplementary aids and services so the student can benefit from special education and participate in the general curriculum;

*they define the general curriculum to be the academic, extracurricular, and other school activities;

*they create a presumption in favor of a general curriculum placement and require the IEP team to justify any other placement; and

*they emphasize transition to adulthood and self-determination by the new provisions that "devolve" or transfer the parent's rights to act for the student to the student him/herself.

2. **The Individualized Education Program Team,** Section 1414(d)(1)(B), consists of

*the student's parents,

*at least one general education teacher of the student, if the student is or may be participating in the general education environment,

*at least one special education teacher or (where appropriate) a provider of special education to the student,

*a representative of the local agency who is qualified to provide or supervise specially designed instruction to meet the unique needs of students with disabilities and is knowledgeable about general curriculum and the availability of local agency resources,

*an individual who can interpret the instructional implications of evaluation results (who may be a member of the team already), and

*at the parents' or agency's discretion, other individuals who have knowledge or special expertise (including related services personnel), and the student (when appropriate).

⌘ *Significance:* The evaluation team and the IEP team have identical members, thus assuring a link between evaluation data and program and placement decisions. More than that, the team members are expert in evaluation, special education programming, special education administration, general education curriculum, and local resources that can support placement into the general education program. By having a team consisting of these individuals, IDEA assures a more robust and holistic evaluation and much better decision-making geared toward "benefit" and the general curriculum.

3. **Parent participation,** Section 1414(f): The LEA must take specific steps to ensure that the student's parent(s) is(are) members of the evaluation and IEP teams. These steps include

   a. advance notice of meetings

   b. mutually convenient scheduling

   c. interpreters when necessary (the parents may have language, sight, or hearing limitations)

   d. meeting without parent participation only where attempts to include parents have failed

   e. allowing parent(s) to participate by telephone

⌘ *Significance:* Each LEA must make a good faith effort to secure parental participation; otherwise, valuable information about the student may not be considered.

4. **Required considerations of IEP,** Section 1414(d)(1)(A). In developing the IEP, the team

    a.   must consider the student's strengths, parents' concerns, and results of all evaluations

    b.   must consider "special factors":

         i.   "in the case of a child whose behavior impedes his or her learning or that of others, (the IEP team must) consider, when appropriate, strategies, including positive behavioral interventions, strategies, and supports to address that behavior";

⌘ *Significance:* The term "impede" is not defined by IDEA and will be defined/operationalized by the IEP team. Moreover, if the student's behavior "impedes," the team must "consider, when appropriate" certain interventions. When would it not be appropriate to consider certain interventions when the behavior impedes the student's learning or that of other students? What must the team consider? It must consider "interventions, including positive behavioral support interventions, strategies, and supports". This phrasing creates a presumption in favor of positive behavioral support interventions, strategies, and supports; they are presumptively favored, but others are not ruled out. What is the purpose of the "consider" requirement? It is to have the team create a program that will prevent the behaviors from occurring or replace them with more appropriate behaviors; the purpose is intervention and prevention so the student can benefit from special education and progress toward the national policy goals. That is why IDEA uses the term "to address that behavior."

        ii.   "in the case of a child with limited English proficiency, consider the language needs of the child as such needs relate to the child's IEP";

⌘ *Significance:* Some children in special education may need bilingual education, too; the IEP team must consider whether bilingual education will benefit the student.

        iii.   "in the case of a child who is blind or visually impaired, provide for instruction in Braille and use of Braille unless the IEP Team determines, after an evaluation of the child's reading and writing skills, needs, and appropriate reading and writing media (including an evaluation of the child's future needs for instruction in Braille or the use of Braille), that instruction in Braille or the use of Braille is not appropriate for the child;" Section 1414(d)(3)(B)(iii).

⌘ *Significance:* This provision creates a presumption in favor of Braille training but it does not mandate it where it would be inappropriate.

iv. for all students and particularly "in the case of a child who is deaf or hard of hearing, consider the child's language and communication needs, opportunities for direct communications with peers and professional personnel in the child's language and communication mode, academic level, and full range of needs, including opportunities for direct instruction in the child's language and communication mode;"

⌘ *Significance:* This provision suggests that children who use similar languages because of their hearing impairments should be "grouped" with each other.

v. for all students, "whether the child requires assistive technology."

⌘ *Significance:* Assistive technology is a related service and can be useful to many students; the IEP team must rule it in or out for each child.

5. **Special Duties of Regular Educator,** Section 1414(d)(3)(C):

"The regular education teacher of the child, as a member of the IEP Team, shall, to the extent appropriate, participate in the development of the IEP of the child, including the determination of appropriate positive behavioral interventions and strategies and the determination of supplementary aids and services, program modifications, and support for school personnel...."

⌘ *Significance:* The general educator not only must participate in the IEP development but especially must attend to the "impede/positive supports" provision and help the team determine what supplementary aids and services and what program modifications are needed by the student and what supports the general educators and special educators need to help the student benefit from participation in the general education program.

6. An SEA or LEA that places a student in a **private school** is still responsible for implementing the student's IEP.

7. The LEA must **establish or revise** the IEP at the beginning of each school year, Section 1414(d)(4)(A)(i), and must review it as necessary but at least annually to assure that IEP goals are being met.

   a. If they are not being met, the LEA must revise the IEP to address

      i. any lack of expected progress by the student toward the annual goals, and in the general curriculum, where appropriate,

      ii. the results of any nondiscriminatory evaluation,

      iii. information about the child provided to or by the parents,

      iv. the student's anticipated future needs, or

      v. any other matters. Section 1414(d)(4).

   b. For a student currently in special education, the LEA must conduct the review early enough to ensure that all revisions are effect by the beginning of the next school year, Section 1414(d)(2)(A).

⌘ *Significance:* In addition to parent and general educator participation, these provisions assure periodic review with a focus on timeliness, access to and benefit from general education, and use of evaluation data.

D. **Early Intervention,** Part C, Sections 1431-1445, are outcome/result oriented, their purposes being, Section 1431—

*"to enhance the development of infants and toddlers with disabilities and to minimize their potential for developmental delay;

*to reduce the educational costs to our society, including our Nation's schools, by minimizing the need for special education and related services after infants and toddlers with disabilities reach school age;

*to minimize the likelihood of institutionalization of individuals with disabilities and maximize the potential for their independently living in society;

*to enhance the capacity of families to meet the special education needs of their infants and toddlers with disabilities; and

*to enhance the capacity of State and local agencies and service

providers to identify, evaluate, and meet the needs of historically underrepresented populations, particularly minority, low-income, inner-city, and rural populations."

⌘ **Significance:** Early intervention has always been outcome-oriented, with the five outcomes being concerned with the child, the family, and the service system. As much if not more than any other declaration of federal policy, Section 1431 proclaims that the nation's goals are to preserve and strengthen the families of children with disabilities and the children themselves, and, at the same time, to develop state and local capacities to serve them. This "dual accommodation" approach—focused on the family and child on the one hand and the system on the other— now characterizes Part B of IDEA (ages 3 - 21).

    E. **Individualized Family Service Plan (IFSP),** Section 1436: The plan "[S]hall be in writing and contain

        1. "a statement of the infant's or toddler's present levels of physical development, cognitive development, communication development, social or emotional development, and adaptive development, based on objective criteria;"

⌘ **Significance:** The IEP is like the IFSP now, in that it is "domain-based" (cognitive, developmental, behavioral, and physical), and is based on objective evaluation data.

        2. "a statement of the family's resources, priorities, and concerns relating to enhancing the development of the family's infant or toddler with a disability;"

⌘ **Significance:** Here, the family becomes the beneficiary of service intervention; it joins the child as a co-beneficiary. Some of the related services available to children ages 3-21 also benefit families, such as school social work, psychological services, and counseling services. Increasingly, schools are expected to benefit the child and the family alike. That is part of the trend toward service-integration.

        3. "a statement of the major outcomes expected to be achieved for the infant or toddler and the family, and the criteria, procedures, and timelines used to determine the degree to which progress toward achieving the outcomes is being made and whether modifications or revisions of the outcomes or services are necessary;"

⌘ **Significance:** Like the IEP, this provision assures accountability for outcomes.

        4. "a statement of specific early intervention services necessary to meet the unique needs of the infant or toddler and the family,

including the frequency, intensity, and method of delivering services;"

5. "a statement of the natural environments in which early intervention services shall appropriately be provided, including a justification of the extent, to any, to which the services will not be provided in a natural environment;"

⌘ *Significance:* This is the "least restrictive environment" provision as applied to infants and toddlers.

6. "the projected dates for initiation of services that the anticipated duration of the services;"

7. "the identification of the service coordinator from the profession most immediately relevant to the infant's or toddler's or family's needs (or who is otherwise qualified to carry out all applicable responsibilities...) who will be responsible for the implementation of the plan and coordination with other agencies and persons;" and

8. "the steps to be taken to support the transition of the toddler with a disability to preschool or other appropriate services."

⌘ *Significance:* Transition is also assisted because the child's IFSP may be the IEP if the parents and LEA consent, Section ***.

F. **IFSP Team includes,** Section 1436—

1. the child's parent(s)

    a. under Section 1436(e), "(t)he contents of the individualized family service plan shall be fully explained to the parents and informed written consent from the parents shall be obtained prior to the provision of early intervention services described in such plan. If the parents do not provide consent with respect to particular early intervention service, then the early intervention services to which consent is obtained shall be provided."

2. other family members as requested by parent when feasible

3. the service coordinator

4. person(s) directly involved in conducting the child and family evaluations and assessments,

5. as appropriate, persons who will provide services to the child and family, and

6.   an advocate or person outside the family, at the parents' request.

Note: If the required persons cannot physically attend, other arrangements must be made to secure their participation.

⌘ *Significance:* Here, the parents and their chosen "allies" are put into the IFSP process, that is, into the decision-making process related to the child's development, from the outset. They will have the IFSP experience when their child becomes eligible for an IEP; their collaboration and advocacy skills will have been honed during the IFSP process; and thus they are launched into the decision-making, collaborative mode from the very beginning. Also, the necessary experts are identified and put into the decision-making process, as in the IEP.

   G. The contents of the IFSP include, Section 1436(a):

      1.   a multidisciplinary assessment of the unique strengths and needs of the infant or toddler and the identification of services appropriate to meet such needs;

⌘ *Significance:* The assessment must be nondiscriminatory, consistent with IDEA Part B and Section 504 of the Rehabilitation Act Amendments of 1975.

      2.   a family-directed assessment of the resources, priorities, and concerns of the family and the identification of the supports and services necessary to enhance the family's capacity to meet the developmental needs of the infant or toddler;

⌘ *Significance:* "Family-directed" is appropriate when the beneficiary of the services is the family, as this provision directs.

      3.   a written individualized family service plan developed by a multidisciplinary team, including the parents.

⌘ *Significance:* Here again the family is a decision-maker.

   H. Timing, Section 1436—

      1.   The initial meeting must be held within 45 days after the child or family is referred to the lead state agency, 34 C.F.R. Section 303.342(a),

      2.   the IFSP must be developed "within a reasonable period of time after the assessment" of the child is complete, Section 1436(c),

      3.   the IFSP "shall be evaluated once a year and the family shall be provided a review of the plan at 6-month intervals or more often

where appropriate based on infant or toddler and family needs", Section 1436(b).

4. "With the parents' consent, early intervention services may commence prior to the completion of the assessment" of the child, Section 1436(c).

⌘ *Significance:* Earlier services are better, even when the full assessment is incomplete; and frequent review is better in light of the usually fast-changing needs of infants and their families.

I. **Related and Other Services and Supports:** Section 1414(d)(1)(A)(iii) requires the IEP team to specify (a) which related services the student needs to benefit from special education, (b) which supplementary aids and services the student needs to participate in and progress through the general curriculum, and (c) what program modifications or supports for school personnel will be provided so the student can participate in and benefit from general and special education.

⌘ *Significance:* This provision marshals a wide range of services to benefit of the student and the school's special and general educators; it thus supports placement in the least restrictive environment, consistent with other IDEA provisions.

Note: The Supreme Court clarified the meaning of a related service in *Irving Independent School District v. Tatro* (1984). There, the Court looked at two crucial factors to determine whether a service is "related" or is "health service" that is not a related service: (a) whether the service in question is a supportive service that enables the student to benefit from special education; and (b) whether the service in question is a medical service serving purposes other than educational diagnosis or evaluation. The Court held that the service in *Tatro*, clean intermittent catheterization, is a supportive service because, without it, the student could not attend school and thereby benefit from special education. Clean intermittent catheterization also is not a medical service because it can be administered by a nurse and school nurses are clearly required by Congress under the "school health service" component of "related services." The test of "related" vs. "medical" service is, in the last analysis, based on whether the service is performed by a person other than a physician or other than under a physician's direct supervision and authority; whether the service is simple, has a low cost but high benefit to the student, is not "merely" life-sustaining but also has educational value, is typically provided in school as distinguished from a hospital, and is performed by a person who may do that service without special licensure or without violating the state laws on medical and nursing practice.

J. Transition services

1. Section 1402(30) defines "transition services" to be "a coordinated set of activities for a student with disabilities that

    a. "is designed within an outcome-oriented process, which promotes movement from school to post-school activities, including post-secondary education, vocational training, integrated employment (including supported employment), continuing adult education, adult services, independent living, or community participation;"

    b. "is based upon the individual student's needs, taking into account the student's preferences and interests;" and

    c. "includes instruction, related services, community experiences, the development of employment, and other post-school adult living objectives, and, when appropriate, acquisition of daily living skills and functional vocational evaluation."

❅ *Significance:* The word "coordinated" means that the services are in sync with each other; there must be more than one service and each service must dovetail with the others. The outcomes are specified (e.g., postsecondary education); employment is preferred to supported employment as indicated by the fact that "supported employment" is in parentheses. Furthermore, the outcomes are "generic" in many respects—the same outcomes as students without disabilities usually are prepared to attain. The transition activities must be based on the student's preferences and thus the student's curriculum should include self-determination instruction and skill-development. The transition curriculum must be community-based and community-referenced, as indicated by the third subsection; the ends or goals are thus connected to the means or curriculum and the transition training is delivered where transition skills are needed (in the community), thus assuring generalizability and durability of skills. Because transition planning is part of the IEP, it must benefit the student; otherwise, it is not appropriate as failing the *Rowley* test of benefit. That is the import of the word "promote."

2. A student's transition plan is part of the student's IEP, Section 1414(d)(1)(A).

3. ("B)eginning at age 14, and updated annually," the student's IEP must contain "a statement of the transition service needs of the child under the applicable components of the child's IEP that focuses on the child's courses of study (such as participation in advanced placement courses or a vocational educational program)", Section 1414(d)(1)(A)(vii)(I).

4. ("B)eginning at age 16 (or younger, if determined appropriate by the IEP Team), a statement of needed transition services for the child, including, when appropriate, a statement of the interagency responsibilities or any needed linkages;" Section 1414(d)(1)(A)(vii)(II).

5. "(B)eginning at least one year before the child reaches the age of majority under State law, a statement that the child has been informed of his or her rights under this title, if any, that will transfer to the child on reaching the age of majority." Section 1414(d)(1)(A)(vii)(III).

6. When appropriate, the student's IEP must include a statement of the interagency responsibilities or linkages (or both) that the student needs before he or she leaves school, Section 1414(d)(1)(A)(vii)(II).

⌘ **Significance:** These subsections are the "devolution" provisions; they provide for the rights of the student's parents to devolve to the student when the student achieves the age of majority (18). They advance the concept of competency of the student (competent by reason of age and capacity to make decisions and participate in shared educational decision-making.)

K. Tuition reimbursement

Note: In *School Committee of the Town of Burlington v. Department of Education of Massachusetts* (1985), the Supreme Court held that IDEA requires local educational agencies to reimburse parents for their expenditures for private placement if the local educational agency does not provide the student an educational benefit but the private school does. The Court based its decision on two factors: (a) the LEA does not provide an appropriate education, but (b) the private school does. The IDEA amendments of 1997 codify the Court's decision but add exceptions and limitations.

1. Section 1412(a)(10)(C)(i) "does not require a local educational agency to pay for the cost of education, including special education and related services, of a child with a disability at a private school or facility if that agency made a free appropriate public education available to the child and the parents elected to place the child in such private school or facility."

⌘ **Significance:** The basic rule of IDEA is that the federal funds will be used for public education; thus "free appropriate public education" (FAPE) is the overall principle of IDEA.

2. Section 1414(a)(10)(DC)(ii) codifies the Court's rule, an exception to the "public" in FAPE: "If the parents of a child with a disability, who previously received special education and related services under the authority of a public agency, enroll the child in a private elementary of secondary school without the consent of or referral by the public agency, a court or a hearing officer may require the agency to reimburse the parents for the cost of that enrollment if the court or hearing officer finds that the agency had not made a free appropriate public education available to the child in a timely manner prior to that enrollment."

3. Section 1414(a)(10)(C)(iii) sets out the limitations on reimbursement, most of which were grafted onto IDEA by various courts before the 1997 amendments: "The cost of reimbursement described [above] may be reduced or denied—

    a. "if—

        i. "at the most recent IEP meeting the parents attended prior to removal of the child from public school, the parents did not inform the IEP team that they were rejecting the placement proposed by the public agency to provide a free appropriate public education to their child, including stating their concerns and their intent to enroll their child in a private school at public expense; or

        ii. "10 business days (including any holidays that occur on a business day) prior to the removal of the child from the public school, the parents did not give written notice to the public agency of the information (that they were rejecting the IEP);

    b. "if, prior to the parents' removal of the child from public school, the public agency informed the parents, through the notice requirements described in Section 1415(b)(7), of its intent to evaluation the child (including a statement of the purpose of the evaluation that was appropriate and reasonable), but the parents did not make the child available for such evaluation; or

    c. "upon judicial finding of unreasonableness with respect to actions taken by the parents."

⌘ *Significance:* These provisions are the essence of fairness: they require the parents to notify the LEA so the LEA may "cure" any default in appropriate education and thus avoid tuition reimbursement.

5. The cost of reimbursement may not be reduced or denied under Section 1414(a)(10)(C)(iv) if:

    a. "the parent is illiterate and cannot write in English;

    b. "compliance with [the no-reimbursement without parental notice] would likely result in physical or serious emotional harm to the child;

    c. "the school prevented the parents from providing such notice; or

    d. "the parents had not received notice" that they had to notify the LEA of their intentions to seek reimbursement.

⌘ *Significance:* These, too, reflect a fairness approach. Illiteracy, danger to the child, or school malfeasance or negligence are excuses to the parental notice requirement.

L. **Additional remedies for violation of "appropriate" education**

    1. **Extended school year services** (ESY) are available to students who may regress or experience significant delays in recouping their progress because they are out of school during the summer. IDEA, as interpreted by many courts, entitles students to receive an appropriate education during summers and/or other periods when the LEA ceases services for its students. The students' IEPs should provide for ESY services. ESY also is an "equitable" remedy (one that is in a court's discretion) that can be imposed by the court in response to a violation of the right to an appropriate education. The right to an appropriate education demands individualized education regardless of predetermined number of school days in any given district.

    2. **Compensatory education,** that is, education over and above that to which the student otherwise would be entitled, typically, beyond the student's 21st birthday or expected graduation date, is available as an equitable remedy. Although not specifically mandated by 1997 amendments, compensatory education is awardable when the LEA denies the student a "basic floor of opportunity" as is the student's right under *Rowley*. The court will consider the length of time that the LEA refused to confer an educational benefit and the consequences of that denial. Both must be "gross" or "flagrant".

⌘ *Significance:* While these remedies are not specifically written into IDEA, they are consistent with and rest on the Supreme Court's tuition reimbursement decision in *Burlington* and, under the theory of individualized access to a basic floor of opportunity, provide additional avenues through which students may receive services if the LEA fails to provide an appropriate education.

IV. Least Restrictive Appropriate Educational Placement

A. **Introduction:** Originally known as "mainstreaming" and now sometimes referred to as "integration" or "inclusion," this requirement has the potential for improving the education of students with disabilities significantly, redressing some of the exclusion from educational opportunities and post-school access that schools have imposed on them and their families, and contributing to the education of all pupils, the training of all educators, and the enlightenment of the public at large. The 1997 significantly enhance the LRE rule and presume that a student will participate in the academic, extracurricular, and other non-academic programs of the LEA.

The word "presume" is important. IDEA enacts a presumption that students with disabilities will be educated in the general curriculum and are to participate in other general education activities. This presumption in favor of inclusion in and progress through the general curriculum has always been part of IDEA; the 1997 amendments, however, give the rule a new focus by linking nondiscriminatory evaluation, IEPs, and other appropriate education provisions to students' access to and progress through the general curriculum and by requiring the accommodations and adjustments necessary for the students to have access to the general curriculum.

This presumption is a "rebuttable presumption". While the presumption is in favor of an LRE placement (that is, integration or inclusion) "to the maximum extent appropriate," the term "appropriate" is defined in relation to each student's individual needs. If LRE (integration or inclusion) is not appropriate for a given student, then the presumption may be rebutted.

Moreover, the LRE rule promotes three public policy values: (a) the value of an appropriate education for students with disabilities; (b) the value of having students with and without disabilities associate with each other, thus removing the stigma of "difference/disability;" and (c) the value of conservation of fiscal capital, it usually being less expensive to operate one school system than two segregated ones.

B. **The general rule** of least restrictive environment is set out in Section 1412(a)(5): "To the maximum extent appropriate, students with disabilities...(will be) educated with students who are not disabled, and special classes, separate schooling or other removal of students with disabilities from the regular educational environment (may occur) only when the nature or severity of the disability of a child is such that education in regular classes with the use of supplementary aids and services cannot be achieved satisfactorily" for that student.

⌘ *Significance:* The presumption is set out here: include unless not appropriate.

C. Section 1414(d)(1)(A)(iv) strengthens the presumption by requiring the student's IEP to contain "an explanation of the extent, if any, to which the child will not participate" with nondisabled children in the regular class and in "the general curriculum" and "extracurricular and other nonacademic activities" (consistent with Section 1414(d)(1)(A)(iii).

⌘ *Significance:* IDEA requires the IEP team to justify any removal from the least restrictive environment and defines the three dimensions of that environment: general academic curriculum, extracurricular activities, and other school activities such as recess, meal-times, transportation, dances, or spectator-sport activities. This section also requires the IEP team to explain "the extent, if any" to which the student will be segregated; thus, it allows for partial inclusion where total inclusion is not appropriate. Finally, the IEP team must consider each dimension listed above and the extent to which the student must be removed for an appropriate education. This provision allows for "mix and match" where total integration is appropriate under one dimension and partial integration is appropriate under another dimension.

D. **Least restrictive environment through nondiscriminatory evaluation and the individualized education program.**

1. The nondiscriminatory evaluation/individualized education program team must evaluate the student and especially focus on evaluation and program that leads to placement in the general curriculum, Section 1414(b)(2)(A).

2. As noted in the section on nondiscriminatory evaluation, a student may not be classified into special education where the "determinant factor" for potential special education classification involves the "lack of instruction in reading or math or limited English proficiency," Section 1414(b)(5).

3. Moreover, the NDE/IEP team must use "a variety of assessment tools and strategies" that "may assist" the team in acquiring "information related to enabling the child to be involved in and progress in the general curriculum or, for preschool children, to participate in appropriate activities," Section 1414(b)((2)(A).

4. In addition, when conducting an initial evaluation or a reevaluation, the team must determine "whether any additions to or modifications to the special education and related services are

needed to enable the child to...participate, as appropriate, in the general curriculum," Section 1414(c)(1)(A)(iv).

5. Next, the student's IEP must contain

    a.   a statement "how the child's disability affects the child's involvement in and progress in the general curriculum," Section 1414(d)(A)(i)(I);

    b.   annual goals, including short-term goals, relating to the child's "involvement and progress in the general curriculum," Section 1414(d)(1)(A)(ii)(I);

    c.   a statement of related services and supplementary aids and services and "a statement of the program modifications or supports for school personnel that will be provided for the child...to be involved and progress in the general curriculum...and to participate in extracurricular and other nonacademic activities," Section 1414(d)(1)(A)(III).

    d.   a statement regarding State and district-wide assessments and whether the student will participate in them, what accommodations the student needs to participate in them, and, if the student is not to participate in them, why and what other assessments the student will undergo, Section 1414(d)(1)(A)(v)(I) and (II).

    e.   The individualized education program team must include a general educator (Section 1414(d)(C)) who has specific duties relating to the student's participation in the general curriculum, namely, to identify the program modifications and supports that advance the LRE placement, Section 1414(d)(1)(B)(ii); and an LEA representative who is "knowledgeable about the general curriculum and...about the availability of resources" of the LEA that can be brought to bear on appropriate education in the least restrictive environment, Section 1414(d)(1)(B)(iv).

    f.   As noted above under "appropriate education" and "transition," the transition components of a student's IEP are on "full participation" outcomes (Section 1402(30)(A)) and their implementation through inclusive methods such as community service, employment and other post-school objectives, Section 1402(30)(C).

⌘ *Significance:* IDEA now defines the general curriculum (academic, extracurricular, and other school activities) and links the student's placement in the general curriculum to the nondiscriminatory evaluation and the individualized education program. Provisions related to the team

42

membership also advance the LRE rule; they require a general educator and a person knowledgeable about resources that can be used to achieve an LRE placement. Last, the transition provisions tie to the student's post-school life in the least restrictive environment that nondisabled adults enjoy.

E. Discipline and the least restrictive environment

1. If disciplined, students have a right to a functional behavioral assessment and positive behavioral support intervention; both must address the behavior for which they are disciplined and whether their behavior jeopardizes their placements in least restrictive environments, Section 1414(k)(1)(B).

2. Moreover, students placed into interim alternative educational settings on account of their behavior retain their rights to access to the general curriculum, Section 1414(k)(3).

3. Finally, the stay-put safeguard is available to retain the least restrictive placement except where the behavior for which the student is disciplined involves weapons or drug violations or dangerous behavior, Sections 1415(k)(7) and 1402(30)(C).

❡ *Significance:* These provisions connect discipline, behavior, and interventions to the least restrictive environment rule. Discipline is no longer a simple justification for removing the student from the LRE placement.

F. The least restrictive environment and Part C of IDEA (0–3)

1. States must put into effect a statewide system of "appropriate early intervention services" (Section 1434(a)(2)) which must be provided in "natural environments" in which infants and toddlers without disabilities would participate, to the extent appropriate for those with disabilities, Section 1436(d)(5).

2. There is a strong preference for integration, for the purpose of Part C is to enhance infants' and toddlers' development by maximizing their potential for independent living, Section 1431(a).

3. The only exception to this preference is in situations where infants or toddlers require extensive medical intervention, Section 1436(d)(5).

❡ *Significance:* Requiring the least restrictive placement during early intervention promotes similar placements as the child grows older. It sets a precedent and an expectation for general education placements and activities.

G. Applicable case law

Three cases stand out as definitive in interpreting the LRE rule. The first, *Roncker v. Walter* (1983), created a "feasibility" or "portability" test: if it is feasible for an LEA to replicate (that is, to "transport") the services a student receives in a more restrictive setting to a less restrictive one and still assure benefit to the student in the more integrated setting, the district must do so. The *Roncker* "feasibility" test uses the LRE doctrine proactively by demanding that the LEA make accommodations and forcing real change in LEA programs

The second case, *Daniel R.R. v. State Board of Education* (1989), set out a two-part test to comply with the presumption in favor of general education placement.

> a. Can education in the general program be achieved satisfactorily with the use of supplemental aids and services?
>
> *Have modifications been implemented?
>
> *Will the student receive an educational benefit from general education?
>
> *Will the student's "overall educational experience" in general education confer other than purely academic benefit?
>
> *What is the effect of the student's placement on the general education environment and the education of other students?
>
> b. If education in the general education classroom cannot be achieved satisfactorily, has integration occurred "to the maximum extent appropriate"?

The third and most recent definitive case, *Board of Education v. Holland* (1992), incorporated the rules of the other two cases and set out a four-part test:

> a. educational benefit to student
>
> b. nonacademic benefit to student
>
> c. "possible negative effects" of general class placement
>
> d. costs involved in accommodating placement

A court is required to consider each of these factors and then, weighing each against the other, determine whether the student has a right to placement in the general curriculum.

Significantly, IDEA explicitly accepts each of these four factors and thus codifies the decision. With respect to the "cost" consideration, it does so by allowing the funds that assure an LRE placement to be used to benefit nondisabled students.

V. Procedural Due Process: Due process consists of the right to protest actions of the SEA or LEA through mediation, appeal to an impartial hearing officer, and appeal to state or federal courts.

⌘ *Significance:* The 1997 amendments continue IDEA's prior protections, including notice, access to records, parent participation and due process hearings. Section 1415, however, adds the opportunity for mediation and imposes new notice obligations on parents and limits their rights with respect to tuition reimbursement.

A. Parental consent

1. An LEA must obtain parental consent the initial and all subsequent evaluations and for the initial placement into special education, Section 1414(a)(1)(C) and (c)(3). As noted above under "nondiscriminatory evaluation," the LEA may go to mediation or due process if the parents refuse consent, and, in the case of reevaluations, they may conduct the reevaluation if they have taken "reasonable" steps to secure parental consent but have been unable to do so.

2. "Consent" as defined in IDEA's regulations (pre-1997 Amendments) means that the parents have been fully informed, in their native language or in another suitable method of communication, of all the information relevant to the activity for which the LEA seeks consent, that the parents understand and agree in writing that the activity may be carried out, that the request for consent describes the activity and lists all records released and to whom, and that the parents understand that their consent is voluntary and may be revoked at any time.

3. Parents' refusal to consent may be overruled only after a due process hearing (or appeal) where hearing officer finds in favor of the LEA, Section 1414(1)(C)(ii).

4. The SEA may assign surrogate parents where the child's parents are unknown or unavailable, Section 1415(b)(2).

$\mathcal{H}$ **Significance:** Parents have a legal and moral duty to their child; the duty requires them to assure that their child is educated (hence, the truancy laws enforceable against parents). Parents also have a legal right to consent or not consent to educational, medical, or similar procedures to which their child will be subjected. IDEA codifies these general rights and at the same time seeks to create, through the parental consent mechanism, a means whereby parents and educators will collaborate and share the decision-making that affects a child's education.

B. General Notice requirements

1. General Notice: An SEA or LEA must give prior written notice to parents, guardians or surrogate parents whenever it "proposes to initiate a change or refuses to initiate or change the identification, evaluation, or educational placement of the child...or the provision of a free appropriate public education to the child", Section 1415(b)(3).

$\mathcal{H}$ **Significance:** This section refers to the notice that the SEA or LEA must given whenever it wants to act or refuses to act. This is a general notice.

2. The general notice "shall include

   "1. a description of the action proposed or refused by the agency;

   "2. an explanation of why the agency proposes or refused to take the action;

   "3. a description of any other options that the agency considered and the reasons why those options were rejected;

   "4. a description of each evaluation procedure, test, record, or report that the agency used as a basis for the proposed or refused action;

   "5. a description of any other factors that are relevant to the agency's proposal or refusal;

   "6. a statement that the parents of a child with a disability have protection under the procedural safeguards... and, if this notice is not an initial referral for evaluation, the means by which a copy of a description of the procedural safeguards can be obtained; and

   "7. sources for parents to contact to obtain assistance in understanding the [provisions in the notice]", Section 1415(c).

46

⌘ Significance: This section requires the SEA or LEA to justify its act. and informs the parents what steps they may take if they disagree with the agency's proposed action, thereby putting them at a more "even table" with the agency.

C. **Procedural Safeguards Notice.** In addition to the general notice, IDEA now provides for a special notice, called the "procedural safeguards notice," whenever an SEA or LEA takes or proposes to take certain action.

1. The procedural safeguards notice "shall be given to the parents, at a minimum—

   "a. upon initial referral for evaluation;

   "b. upon each notification of an individualized education program meeting and upon reevaluation of the child; and

   "c. upon registration of a complaint" by a parent, Section 1415(d)(1).

2. The procedural safeguards notice "shall include a full explanation of the procedural safeguards, written in the native language of the parents, unless it clearly is not feasible to do so, and written in an easily understandable manner... relating to—

   "a. independent educational evaluation (see also Section 1415(b)(1);

   "b. prior written notice;

   "c. parental consent;

   "d. access to educational records;

   "e. opportunity to present complaints;

   "f. the child's placement during pendency of due process proceedings;

   "g. procedures for students who are subject to placement in an interim alternative educational setting;

   "h. requirements for unilateral placement by parents of children in private schools at public expense;

   "i. mediation;

47

    "k. due process hearings, including requirements for disclosure of evaluation results and recommendations;

    "l. State-level appeals (if applicable in that State);

    "l. civil actions; and

    "m. attorneys' fees", Section 1415(d)(2).

⌘ *Significance:* The procedural safeguards notice gives the parents even more specific information than the general notice and relates essentially to all of the child's IDEA rights and how the parents can enforce those rights. Congress clearly intends that there will be no uninformed parents and that the SEA and LEA will make a full disclosure of IDEA rights.

    D. **Complaints** (requests for due process hearings).

        1. Parents or their attorney may file a complaint against the SEA or LEA with respect to "any matter relating to the identification, evaluation, or educational placement of the child, or the provision of a free appropriate public education to such child", Section 1415(b)(6).

        2. When they file a complaint, the parents or their attorney must provide notice ("which shall remain confidential") to the SEA or LEA regarding the complaint and must set out in the notice the following:

          "i. the name of the child, the address of the residence of the child, and the name of the school the child is attending;

          "ii. a description of the nature of the problem of the child relating to such proposed initiation or change, including facts relating to such problem; and

          "iii. a proposed resolution of the problem to the extent known and available to the parents at the time", Section 1415(b)(7)(B).

⌘ *Significance:* The parents' notice prevents the parents from catching the SEA or LEA unawares. It thereby allows the SEA or LEA to "cure" or attempt to cure any problems that the parents identify and to know (in advance of mediation or a due process hearing) exactly the nature of the parents' complaint and what they want the agency to do (the remedy they seek).

E. Mediation

1. The SEA must "allow" parents and the SEA or LEA "to resolve (their) disputes through a mediation process which, at a minimum, shall be available whenever a (due process) hearing is requested," Section 1415(e)(1).

⌘ *Significance:* Recognizing that due process hearings and appeals to a court, with the subsequent trial of a case, both reflects and exacerbates miscommunication (and perhaps more) between the parents and the SEA or LEA and hoping to forestall those factors and to preserve collaborative decision-making between the parents and the SEA or LEA, Congress made mediation an option for parents and the SEA or LEA, Section 1415(e). The phrase "at a minimum" means that mediation can be made available before a dispute results in a complaint and request for a due process hearing.

2. The mediation procedures "shall ensure that the mediation process (i) is voluntary on the part of the parties; (ii) is not used to deny or delay a parent's right to a due process hearing...or to deny any other rights" under IDEA, and (iii) is conducted by a qualified and impartial mediator who is trained in effective mediation techniques," Section 1415(e)(2)

⌘ *Significance:* Mediation may precede a due process hearing but, since justice delayed is justice denied, it must not get in the way of the parent's request for a hearing.

3. If the parents "choose not to use the mediation process," the SEA must have in place a process for them to "meet, at a time and location convenient to the parents, with a disinterested party...to encourage the use, and explain the benefits, of the mediation process," Section 1415(e)(2(B).

⌘ *Significance:* The parents may not be compelled to mediate but their decision to not mediate should at least be well informed.

4. The SEA bears the entire fiscal responsibility for the mediation process, Section 1415(e)(2)(D).

⌘ *Significance:* Because neither the LEA nor parents bear any costs associated with mediation, they have no fiscal disincentive to avoid it.

5. The mediation itself must be scheduled "in a timely manner and...held in a location...convenient to the parties" and any agreement reached in mediation "shall be set forth in a written mediation agreement" but "(d)iscussions that occur during the mediation process shall be confidential and may not be used as evidence in any subsequent due process hearings or civil

roceedings and the parties to the mediation may be required to a confidentiality pledge prior to the commencement of (due) ∠ss (hearings)," Section 1415(e)(2)(E), (F), and (G).

⌐ance: Mediation should be simple, frank, and nonprejudicial ⌐earings; this is the norm for mediation outside of IDEA.

F. Due process hearings

1. Parents have a right to an "impartial due process hearing" to be conducted by the SEA or LEA, Section 1415(f)(1). (Note: An SEA or LEA also may request a hearing.)

2. "At least five days" before the hearing, the parents and agency "shall disclose to all other parties all evaluations completed by that date and recommendations based on the offering party's evaluations that the party intends to use at the hearing," Section 1415(f)(2). If the parents or agency refuse to make the required disclosure, the hearing officer "may bar (the noncomplying party) from introducing relevant evaluation or recommendation at the hearing without the consent of the other party," Section 1415(f)(2).

⌘ *Significance:* This provision, like the notice that the parents and agency must give each other about the complaints they have against each other, prevents "surprise" by allowing each party to "discover" the other's evaluation evidence.

3. The hearing officer must be impartial and may not be "an employee of the State educational agency or the local educational agency involved in the care of the child," Section 1415(f)(3).

4. At the hearing, which must be held within 45 days after it is requested and in a place and time convenient to the parties and which may be closed to the public at the parents' option, the parents and agency have the right to "be accompanied and advised by counsel and by individuals with special knowledge or training with respect to the problems of children with disabilities; ... to present evidence and confront, cross-examine, and compel the attendance of witnesses;...to a written, or, at the option of the parents, electronic verbatim record of (the) hearing...(and)...findings of fact and decisions," Section 1415(h).

⌘ *Significance:* The "special knowledge or training" provision disqualifies attorneys but allows others as aides to the parents.

5. Any "aggrieved" party (the "losing party") may appeal from the local hearing officer to the state-level hearing officer and thence to a federal or state court, Section 1415(g) and (i).

6. A court may award "reasonable" attorneys' fees if the parents "prevail" at the state-level hearing or at a court-level hearing or appeal, but the fees are subject to various limitations, Section 1415(i)(3).

⌘ *Significance:* The procedures and criteria for awarding attorneys' fees are now set out by IDEA, whereas that was not the case before the 1997 amendments. The new provisions prevent a court from making arguably unconscionable fee awards.

7. While any local or state due process hearing is pending or while an appeal is pending in a federal or state court (at the trial or appeal level), the student is protected by the "stay put" rule (discussed above under "discipline").

VI. Parent Participation and Shared Decision Making

⌘ *Significance:* One of the original (1975) purposes of IDEA and one of its continuing purposes (under the 1997 Amendments) is protect children's rights and those of their parents or guardians, Section 1401(d)(1)(B).

A. Parents' rights to two different kinds of notice (the general and the procedural safeguards notice) are set out under "due process," above.

B. Students' records are held confidential (not accessible except on a need-to-know basis) but are accessible to parents and educators who need them in order to provide a free appropriate public education to the students.

1. Confidentiality of student records including "any personally identifiable data, information, and records collected or maintained by the State and local educational agencies..." must be assured by the SEA and LEA, Section 1417(c) and Section 1412(a)(8).

2. Parents, however, have access, so

a. the SEA and LEA must have a procedure which includes "an opportunity for the parents of a child with a disability to examine all records relating to such child...", Section 1415(b)(1).

b. the SEA and LEA are both subject to the Family Educational Rights and Privacy Act (FERPA), which is codified at 20 U.S.C. Section 1232g, with regulations at 34 C.F.R., Part 99.

i. FERPA requires the SEAs and LEAs to give parents, guardians and some pupils access to their own student records.

  ii. if the parents wish to challenge the contents of the records, they must be given an opportunity for a hearing.

  iii. FERPA also relates to confidentiality as certain parts of the record may not be released without parental consent.

C. "Family systems" approach throughout IDEA.

 1. Some related services are available directly to families, such as psychological, social work, and counseling services.

 2. For children ages 3 through 5, additional services may be incorporated into the individualized family service plan (IFSP) (see "appropriate education," above).

⌘ *Significance:* The "family systems" approach follows the theory that whatever benefits the child will benefit the child's family (and vice versa).